The Easy Keyboard Library

# Cliff Richard

## 15 classic songs for Keyboard

GW00501974

Published 2001

**Editorial & Production** Anna Joyce
**Design & Art Direction** Dominic Brookman

Music arranged & processed by Barnes Music Engraving Ltd East Sussex TN34 1HA
Cover Image by Redferns Music Picture Library

# Bachelor Boy

Words and Music by Bruce Welch and Cliff Richard

**Suggested Registration:** Electric Guitar / Strings
**Rhythm:** Jazz Waltz
**Tempo:** ♩ = 180

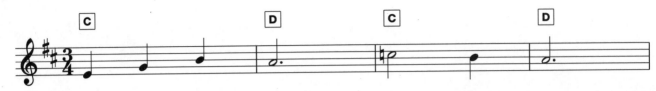

When I was young___ my fa - ther said

'Son I have some - thing to say'.

And what he told me I'll

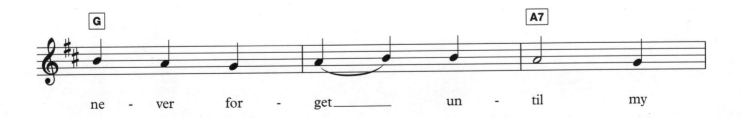

ne - ver for - get___ un - til my

# Congratulations

Words and Music by Bill Martin and Phil Coulter

**Suggested Registration:** Vibraphone / Glockenspiel
**Rhythm:** Swing
**Tempo:** ♩ = 180

# DEVIL WOMAN

Words and Music by Terry Britten and Christine Holmes

**Suggested Registration:** Pop Organ / Guitar
**Rhythm:** 8 Beat or Disco
**Tempo:** ♩ = 112

She's just a de - vil wo - man, with e - vil on her mind. __

Be - ware the de - vil wo - man, she's gon - na get you.

She's just a de - vil wo - man, with e - vil on her mind. __

Be - ware the de - vil wo - man, she's gon - na get you from be -

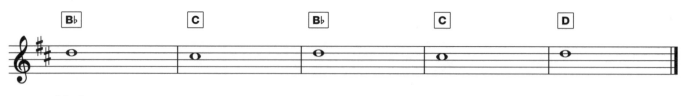

- hind.

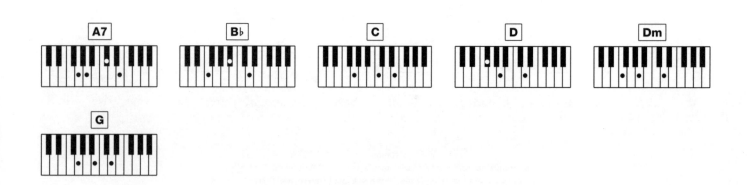

# From A Distance

Words and Music by Julie Gold

**Suggested Registration:** Electric Piano
**Rhythm:** Rock Ballad / 16 Beat
**Tempo:** ♩ = 68

From a dis-tance the world looks blue and__ green, and the

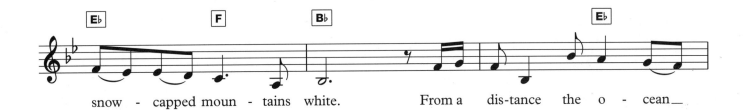

snow - capped moun - tains white. From a dis-tance the o - cean__

meets the stream, and the ea - gle takes to__ flight. From a dis-tance there is__ har-

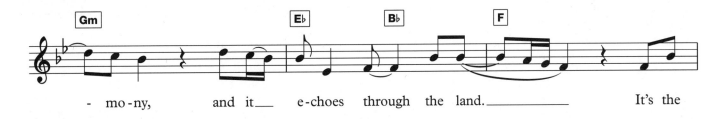

- mo-ny, and it__ e-choes through the land._____ It's the

voice of hope, it's the voice of peace, it's the voice of__ ev - e - ry - man.

From a dis-tance we__ all__ have e - nough, and no - one__ is in

# I Just Don't Have The Heart

Words and Music by Mike Stock, Matt Aitken and Pete Waterman

**Suggested Registration:** Electric Piano / Saxophone
**Rhythm:** Disco or 8 Beat
**Tempo:** ♩ = 125

All a-long the line_____ I've been true to you,_____

ev-en though for some_ time, I know we___ were through. I was feel - in'

our love had end - ed, can't be mend-ed but I can't bear to see you cry.

The feel-ing's gone, it's been miss-ing too long, but I just don't have the heart, I

just don't have the heart to tell you. It's such a shame that it's

end-ing this way,_ but I just don't have the heart, I just don't have the heart to tell you.

# LIVING DOLL

Words and Music by Lionel Bart

**Suggested Registration:** 12 String Guitar
**Rhythm:** Pop Swing
**Tempo:** ♩ = 112

Got my-self a cry - ing, talk - ing, sleep - ing, walk - ing,

liv-ing doll, got to do my best to please her just 'cause she's a

liv-ing doll, such a rov-ing eye, and that is why she sa - tis -

- fies my soul, got the one an' on - ly walk-ing, talk-ing, liv-ing doll.

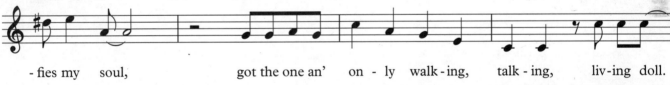

Take a look at her hair, it's real, and if you don't be -

- lieve what I say, just feel, I'm gon-na lock her up in a trunk, so

# MISTLETOE AND WINE

Words and Music by Keith Strachan, Jeremy Paul and Leslie Stewart

**Suggested Registration:** Acoustic Guitar / Strings
**Rhythm:** Waltz
**Tempo:** ♩ = 132

The child is a_____ king, the

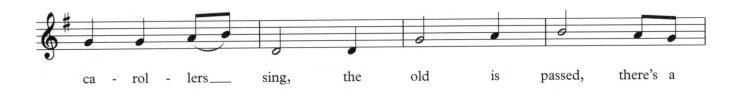

ca - rol - lers___ sing, the old is passed, there's a

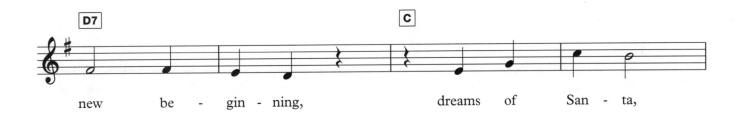

new be - gin - ning, dreams of San - ta,

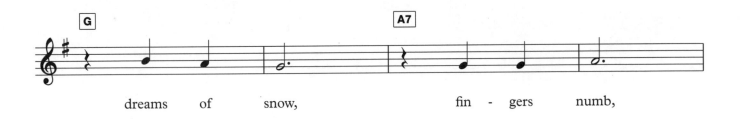

dreams of snow, fin - gers numb,

fa - ces a - glow. It's Christ - mas

time, mis - tle - toe and wine,

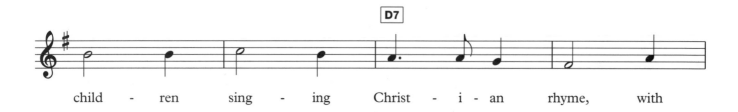

child - ren sing - ing Christ - i - an rhyme, with

logs on the fire,_____ and gifts on the tree, a

time to re - joice in the good that we see.

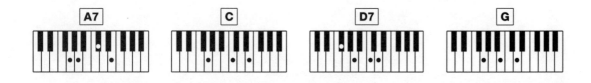

# Please Don't Fall In Love

*Words and Music by Mike Batt*

**Suggested Registration:** Electric Piano / Oboe
**Rhythm:** 8 Beat
**Tempo:** ♩ = 96

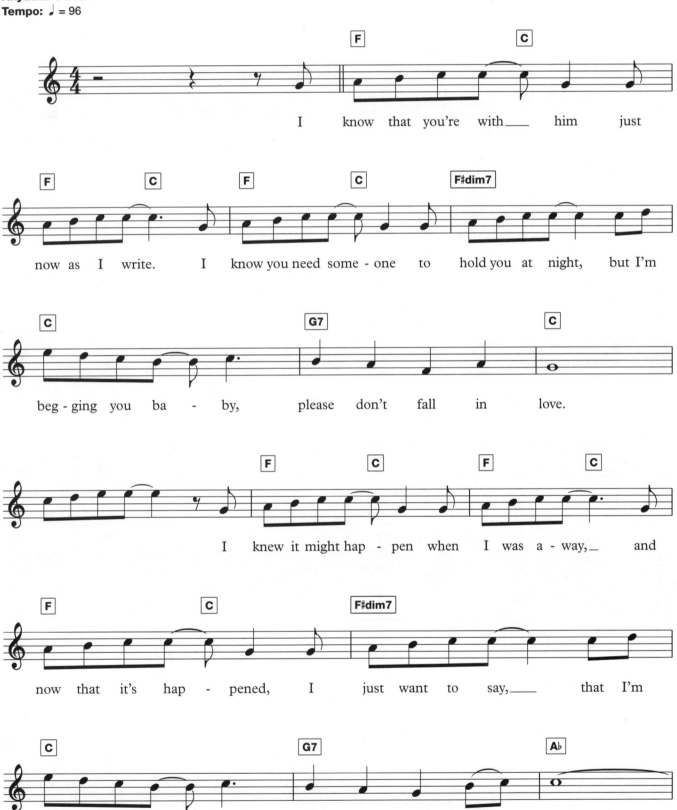

I know that you're with____ him just now as I write. I know you need some-one to hold you at night, but I'm beg-ging you ba - by, please don't fall in love.

I knew it might hap-pen when I was a-way,____ and now that it's hap-pened, I just want to say,____ that I'm beg-ging you ba - by, please don't fall in____ love.____

# My Pretty One

Words and Music by Alan Tarney

**Suggested Registration:** Pop Organ / Glockenspiel
**Rhythm:** Disco
**Tempo:** ♩ = 140

# She's So Beautiful

Words and Music by Hans Poulsen

**Suggested Registration:** Brass / Piano
**Rhythm:** 8 Beat
**Tempo:** ♩ = 140

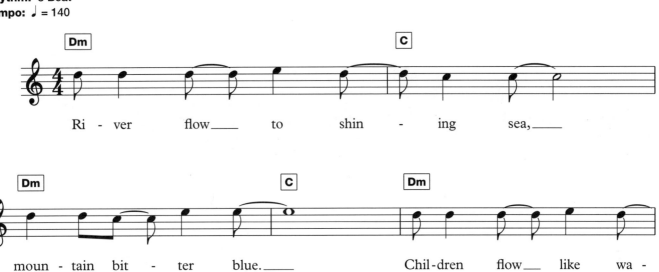

Ri - ver flow___ to shin - ing sea,___

moun - tain bit - ter blue.___ Chil-dren flow___ like wa -

- ter falls,___ sweet our love___ re - new.___

Peace and war___ and love___ a - gain,___ trial and er - ror true.

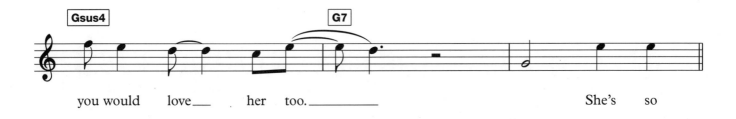

___ Oh, if you were___ to vi - sit there,___

you would love___ her too.___ She's so

beau - ti - ful,___ she's so kind and free,___

she's so beau - ti - ful,___ she's all_____ there is___ to me.___

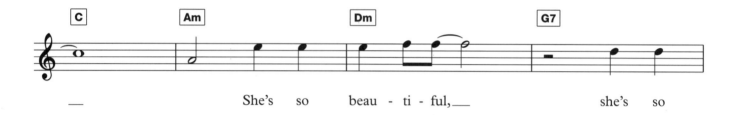

___ She's so beau - ti - ful,___ she's so

kind and free,__ she's so beau - ti - ful,___ she's all___

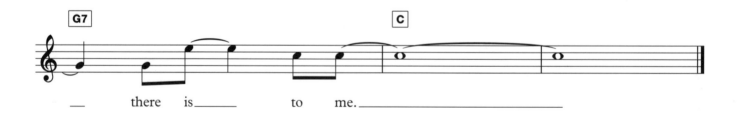

__ there is_____ to me._____

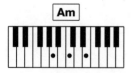
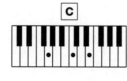
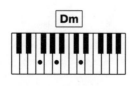

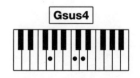

# SOME PEOPLE

Words and Music by Alan Tarney

**Suggested Registration:** 12 String Guitar / Solo Flute
**Rhythm:** 8 Beat
**Tempo:** ♩ = 120

Some peo-ple they tease one an-oth-er, take

pride in them-selves, keep-ing the oth-er one down, well I'm

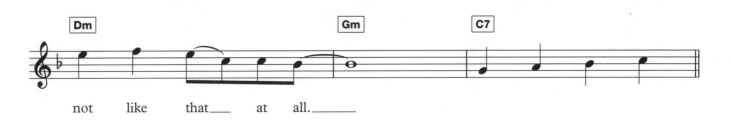

not like that___ at all._____

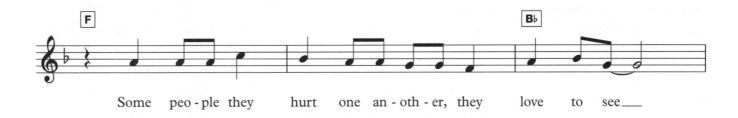

Some peo-ple they hurt one an-oth-er, they love to see___

hurt in the oth-er one's eyes, well I'm not like that__ at all.___

Some peo-ple are born for each-oth-er, they

# Summer Holiday

Words and Music by Bruce Welch and Brian Bennett

**Suggested Registration:** Vibraphone
**Rhythm:** Pop Swing
**Tempo:** ♩ = 108

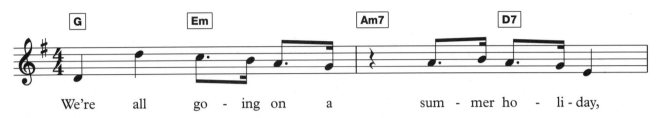

We're all go-ing on a sum-mer ho-li-day,

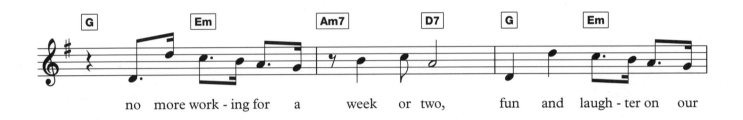

no more work-ing for a week or two, fun and laugh-ter on our

sum-mer ho-li-day, no more__ wor-ries for me or you

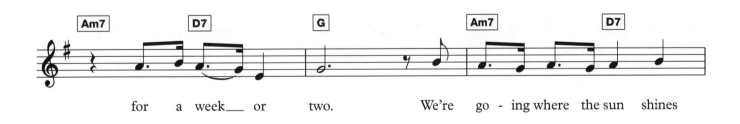

for a week__ or two. We're go-ing where the sun shines

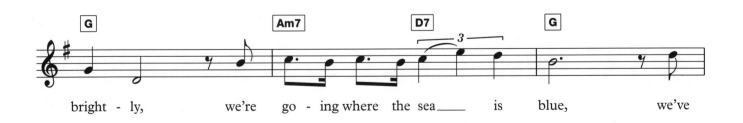

bright-ly, we're go-ing where the sea__ is blue, we've

seen it_____ in the_____ mov - ies, now let's see if it's

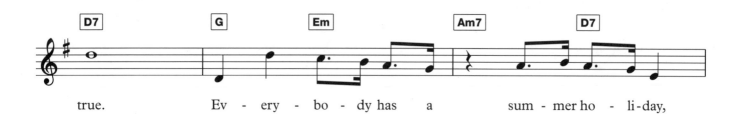

true. Ev - ery - bo - dy has a sum - mer ho - li-day,

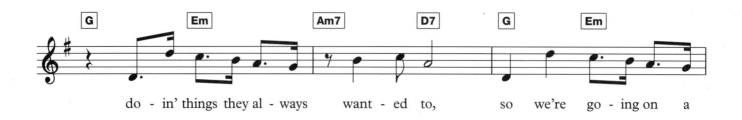

do - in' things they al - ways want - ed to, so we're go - ing on a

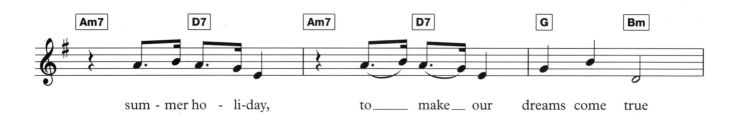

sum - mer ho - li-day, to_____ make__ our dreams come true

for __ me __ and you, for __ me __ and you.

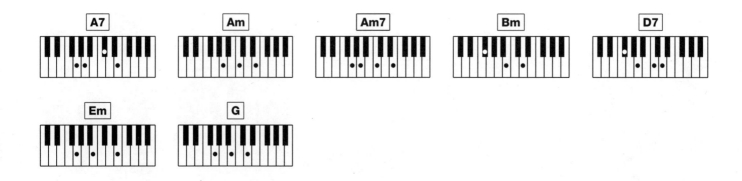

# TRAVELLIN' LIGHT

Words and Music by Sid Tepper and Roy C Bennett

**Suggested Registration:** Saxophone
**Rhythm:** Bounce
**Tempo:** ♩ = 125

Got no bags and bag-gage to slow me down, _____

_ I'm trav-'lin' so fast _ my feet ain't touch-in' the

ground. _____ Tra-vel-in' light, _____ tra-vel-in'

light. _____ Well I just can't wait to

be with my ba-by to-night. _

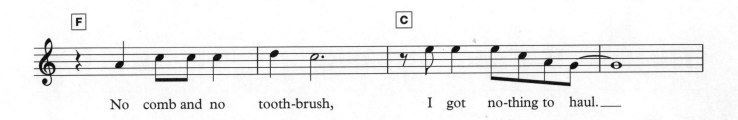

No comb and no tooth-brush, I got no-thing to haul. _

# We Don't Talk Anymore

Words and Music by Alan Tarney

**Suggested Registration:** Electric Guitar / Brass
**Rhythm:** 8 Beat
**Tempo:** ♩ = 128

Used to think that life was sweet,___ used to think we were so___ ___ com - plete,_____ I can't be - lieve___ you'd throw it a - way. ___ Used___ to feel we had it made,___ used to feel we could sail___ a - way,_____ can you i - ma - gine how I feel to - day?___ Well it seems ___ a long time a - go_____ you were the lone - ly one, now___ it comes to let - ting go___ you are the

# The Young Ones

Words and Music by Roy Bennett and Sid Tepper

**Suggested Registration:** Electric Guitar / Pop Organ
**Rhythm:** 8 Beat
**Tempo:** ♩ = 130

# THE EASY KEYBOARD LIBRARY

## Also available in the series

### THE TWENTIES
including:

Ain't Misbehavin'
Ain't She Sweet?
Baby Face
The Man I Love

My Blue Heaven
Side By Side
Spread A Little Happiness
When You're Smiling

### THE THIRTIES
including:

All Of Me
A Fine Romance
I Wanna Be Loved By You
I've Got You Under My Skin

The Lady Is A Tramp
Smoke Gets In Your Eyes
Summertime
Walkin' My Baby Back Home

### THE FORTIES
including:

Almost Like Being In Love
Don't Get Around Much Any More
How High The Moon
Let There Be Love

Sentimental Journey
Swinging On A Star
Tenderly
You Make Me Feel So Young

### THE FIFTIES
including:

All The Way
Cry Me A River
Dream Lover
High Hopes

Magic Moments
Mister Sandman
A Teenager In Love
Whatever Will Be Will Be

### THE SIXTIES
including:

Cabaret
Happy Birthday Sweet Sixteen
I'm A Believer
The Loco-motion

My Kind Of Girl
Needles And Pins
There's A Kind Of Hush
Walk On By

### THE SEVENTIES
including:

Chanson D'Amour
Hi Ho Silver Lining
I'm Not In Love
Isn't She Lovely

Save Your Kisses For Me
Take Good Care Of My Baby
We've Only Just Begun
You Light Up My Life

### THE EIGHTIES
including:

Anything For You
China In Your Hand
Everytime You Go Away
Golden Brown

I Want To Break Free
Karma Chameleon
Nikita
Take My Breath Away

### THE NINETIES
including:

Crocodile Shoes
I Swear
A Million Love Songs
The One And Only

Promise Me
Sacrifice
Think Twice
Would I Lie To You?

Printed in England
The Panda Group · Haverhill · Suffolk · 05/01